1

Collins

# DigiTech

Manasi Kashikar
Sneha Krishnan

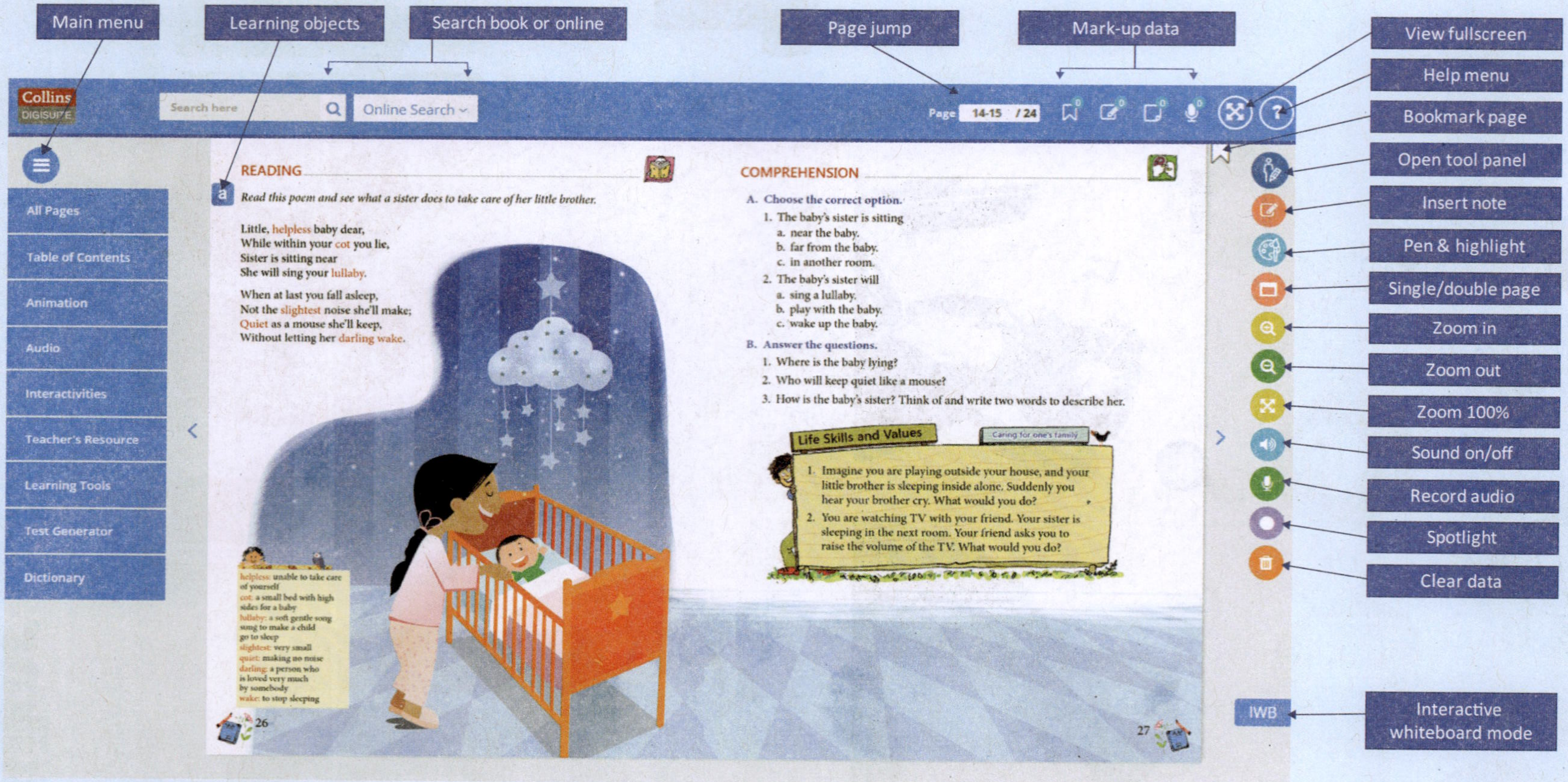


## Student + Teacher

**a** animations

**ilt** instructor-led tutorials

**ia** activities

**w** worksheets

audio

**g** games

**v** videos

## Teacher-only

**lp** lesson plans

**w** worksheets

**tn** teacher's notes

**ak** answer keys

# PREFACE

Over the last few decades, technology has touched almost all aspects of our lives. As technology continues to evolve more rapidly than ever, users are learning newer ways of harnessing the power of technology in their daily lives. In India, easy access to smartphones and affordable internet services have put the power of technology in the hands of millions.

In this backdrop, we believe, it is important for students to:

- ✓ Understand that technology is going to keep evolving. As citizens of the digital world that we all inhabit, keeping abreast of the latest advances is no longer optional, rather, it is an essential life skill.
- ✓ Appreciate that coding skills are as essential today as basic literacy and numeracy. This has been emphasized in the National Educational Policy of 2020 as well.
- ✓ Understand that technology is pervasive and they need to be able to comprehend its intersection with other disciplines. In other words, they need to learn to use technology as a tool to achieve a goal.
- ✓ Take control of regulating their usage and make constructive use of their access to computer devices.

While authoring this series, we have designed and presented the content with the intent of helping students in developing the skills described above. We have ensured that the topics are covered in a relatable manner and that the exercises are practical and applicable. The textbook along with its resources for teachers will enable them to deliver this subject effectively, while keeping the students engaged and interested.

In addition to the curriculum imperatives, we have included concepts as outlined in the National Education Policy 2020. Every grade has computational thinking–based practice problems that are aligned to Bloom's Taxonomy. Topics such as coding and app development have been given their due consideration as their relevance increases in the real world and while making career choices. Artificial intelligence has been woven into the chapters in an age-appropriate manner in the form of Fun with AI boxes, with the intent of enabling students to understand key concepts and applications of AI.

The series equips students with not only the skills required to excel in technology and make the most of it, but also exposes them to the practical applications of these in the world around them.

We would like to thank our intern Sejal Gupta in helping us shape the content.

# KEY FEATURES

**After reading this chapter, I will be able to:**

- ✔ Tell why we use a computer.
- ✔ List the different uses of a computer.
- ✔ Explain the uses of a computer at different places.

Well-defined learning objectives that are mapped to the curriculum to help students identify the topics they will read about in the chapter

Activities and discussions based on real-life situations to set the context for what students are about to learn

**Brainstorm and explore!**

Life Skills

Look at the following pictures. Tick (✔) the activities you can perform with the help of a computer.

**Soak up!**

Computer is a device that takes instructions from the user, stores and processes it, and shows the result.

Additional information/facts about the topic being taught

Contextual meaning of difficult words

**Maintaining Correct Posture**

What will happen if you keep your hand up in the air for more than 10 minutes?

Our body parts ache if we do not use them in the right manner or over-stretch them. Similarly, while working on a computer, it is important to maintain the correct posture.

**posture**: the position of the different parts of the body while sitting, walking and standing

**Crank up!**

Technology Literacy

Emails are electronic mails. We can send or receive information using emails. Both the parties should have an email account to send and receive emails.

Tips and shortcut tricks for the topics covered in the chapter to foster inquiry- and discovery-based learning

**Clear up!**

Can you think of some more places where computers are used?

Hands-on tasks for revision, based on the application of the concept taught

**Brush up!**

Name some activities that you have done using computers.

______________________________

______________________________

Short questions to reinforce the concept learned and promote competency-based learning

Recapitulates all the important points covered in the chapter

### Today I learned!

- Machines are human-made things. They can perform many tasks easily and quickly.
- A computer is a machine that helps us do many things.
- A computer is a device that takes instructions from the user, stores and processes it, and shows the result.
- A computer has a lot of features that makes it a smart machine.
- A PC or desktop computer is placed on a desk.
- A desktop computer has four parts monitor, CPU, keyboard and mouse.
- A lightweight computer that can be placed on our lap is called a laptop.

Revision exercises comprising a blend of both objective and long-answer questions, including both fact- and application-based questions in a variety of formats

### Revise and polish!

Learning Skills

**1. Tick (✔) the correct answer.**

a. Tick the machine that can be placed on a desk.

(i)  ☐ (ii)  ☐

(iii)  ☐ (iv)  ☐

Experiential Learning

### Lab Activities

1. Practice all the dos and don'ts while using a computer in the lab.
2. While exiting the computer lab, ensure the classmate next to you has switched off the computer properly. All students should look at the next classmate's computer to check if it has been shut down properly.

Based on the practical application of the concepts taught to enhance comprehension and provide opportunities for peer tutoring

Practical applications of the concepts covered to help analyse and understand real-world situations, with some extra effort put into research and information gathering

### Project

In groups of two, discuss the many uses of computers in your daily lives.

### Worksheet 1 (Chapters 1 and 2)

Technology Literacy | Art Integration

**1. Answer the following questions in one word.**

a. Name the place where a computer is used for students to study. ____________

b. Name the place where a computer is used to deposit money. ____________

c. Name an activity for which you use a computer. ____________

d. Which machine do you use the most? ____________

e. Name any one machine you have in your study room. ____________

f. Name the place where your dad uses a computer. ____________

Chapter-based revision worksheets focused on competency-based learning and one dedicated worksheet on developing computational thinking through playing games and problem-solving

# NEP IN DIGI TECH

These are some of the key skills that you will see occurring throughout the books at various stages.

**21st Century Skills**

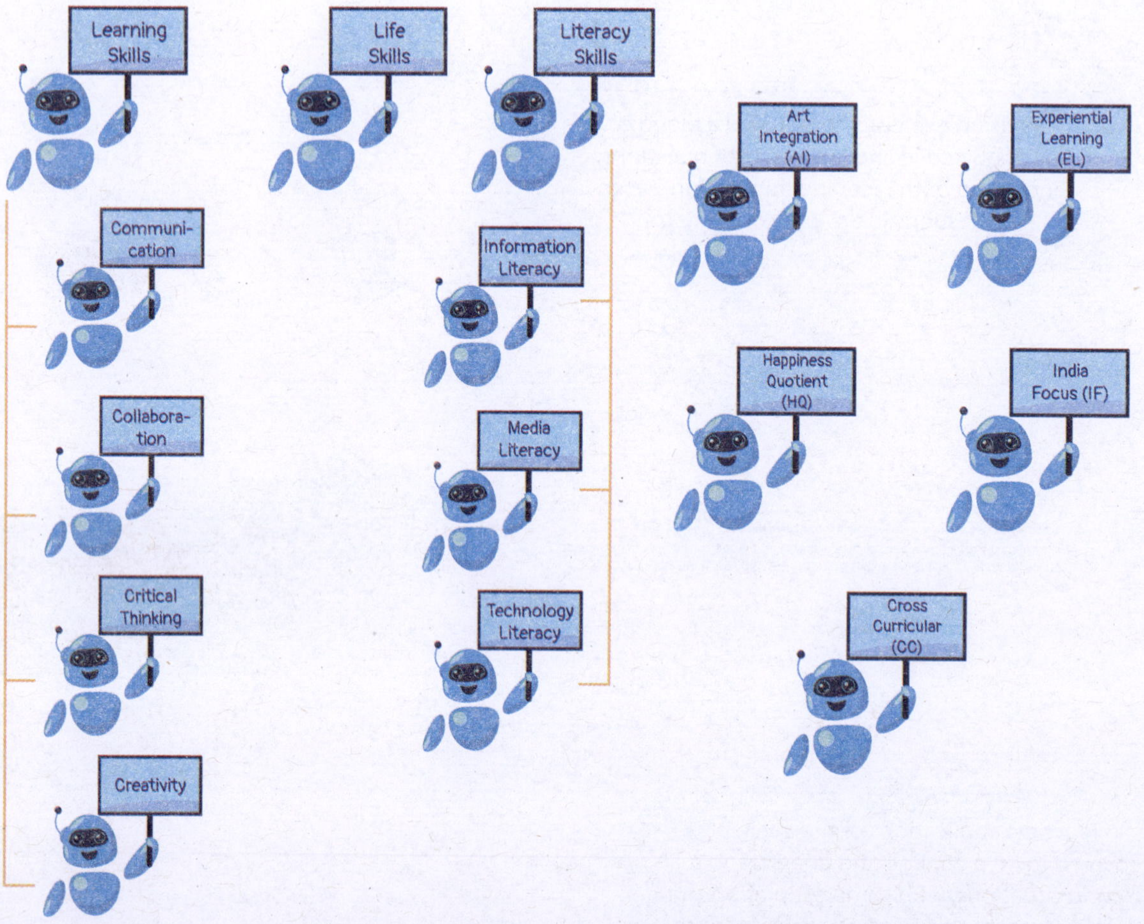


# ABOUT THE AUTHORS

**Sneha Krishnan** and **Manasi Kashikar**, techies at heart, bond over their love of coding. They are co-founders of the company *MindChamp* where they teach coding to school students using fun, activity-based learning. They both love to teach students and that reflects in their work. Together with a team of educators, they have taught thousands of students to create computer games and websites. They want to make coding accessible to young students as well, so they are better equipped for the future.

# CONTENTS

Chapter

1

# Computer—A Machine

## After reading this chapter, I will be able to

- ✔ Differentiate between human-made things and natural things.
- ✔ List objects in my surroundings.
- ✔ Define a computer.
- ✔ List the features of a computer.
- ✔ Compare a laptop with a desktop computer.

## Brainstorm and explore!

**Look at the pictures. Read the uses of these. Write their names in the given space.**

1. It tells us, it is time to go to class.

_______________

2. It cools down our rooms.

_______________

3. We play on it with our friend.

_______________

4. It keeps our things safe.

_______________

5. It helps us talk to people in far-off places.

_______________

6. It takes us from one place to another.

_______________

# Human-made Things and Natural Things

The things made by humans are called human-made things. Machines, clothes, books, etc., are made by humans. Things present in nature are called natural things. Animals, trees and rivers are examples of natural things.

## Brush up!

Look at the following pictures. Write 'H' for human-made things and 'N' for natural things in the given box.

1. 

☐

2. 

☐

3. 

☐

4. 

☐

5. 

☐

6. 

☐

# Machines

A long time ago, we only used to grow food. We did not have any tools to help us. Even simple tasks took a lot of time and effort. Then, we learned to make tools to make our tasks easy. For example, the wheel allowed us to make different means of transport. Today, be it cars or bicycles, wheels are used in many modes of transportation. Figure 1.2 shows how wheels have been used in different modes of transportation.

**Fig. 1.1** | *The first wheel*

**Fig. 1.2** | *Different uses of wheels*

There were many more inventions that helped reduce human effort and perform many tasks easily. We named them **machines**!

A set of parts, which work together to perform a task and reduce human effort, makes a machine.

A clock helps us to be on time. But, is it a machine? Do you know what each part of the clock does?

| Part | What it does | What they do together |
|---|---|---|
| Hour hand | Points to the hour of the day. | Show us the time! |
| Minute hand | Points to the minute of the hour. | |
| Battery | Gives power to the hands. | |

**Fig. 1.3** | *A clock*

## Features of Machines

These are the common features of machines

1. They are made of many parts.
2. They are human-made.
3. They help us perform a particular task.
4. Some machines use electricity to work.

Machines make our lives easy and comfortable. Which machine do we use if we have to

- do maths homework?
- add and subtract numbers?
- search information about anything in the world?
- draw a picture and save it?

A computer can do all these things!

**Crank up!** (Technology Literacy)

All computers are machines but not all machines are computers!

# Enter the World of Computers!

Look around you. Computers are very common and are used almost everywhere.

- Schools use computers to store information about their students and teachers and prepare exam timetables.
- Railway stations and airports use computers to track all trains and aeroplanes.
- At home, computers are used to play games, listen to music, watch movies and search for information.

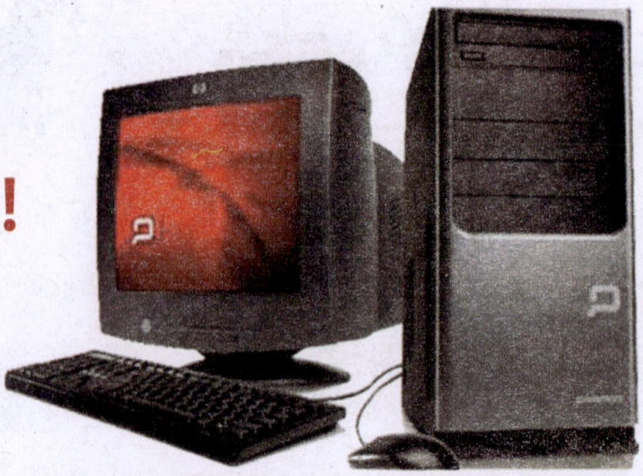

**Fig. 1.4** | *A computer system*

A computer is a smart machine used to perform different tasks. It needs electricity to run.

**Brush up!**

Just like pencils, computers are also made by different companies. Write down the names of three companies that make computers.

______________________________

______________________________

# Features of a Computer

A computer has a lot of features that make it a smart machine.

**Soak up!**

Computer is a device that takes instructions from the user, stores and processes it, and shows the result.

- A computer is very fast.

- A computer is always correct.

- A computer can store a lot of information.

- A computer never gets tired.

- A computer never forgets anything.

- A computer can do many things at the same time.

- A computer has no emotions and feelings.

- A computer always follows the instructions given by the user.

**instructions**: clear and detailed information on how to do something

### Brush up!

Do you see a computer in the following places? If yes, find out what they do.

1. In an ice-cream store
2. In the school
3. At the airport

# Types of Computers

Computers come in different sizes. They can be big, medium or small in size.

## Desktop Computer

A computer system that we place on the desk is called a Desktop Computer. It is also known as **P**ersonal **C**omputer or **PC**.

A desktop computer is heavy. It consists of monitor, CPU, keyboard and mouse.

**Fig. 1.5** | *Desktop computer*

## Laptop

A **laptop** is a portable form of a desktop computer. It is named as laptop because it is compact in such a way that it can be placed on a lap. It is small in size and light in weight. We can carry it from one place to another. The mouse on a laptop is called **touchpad** or trackpad.

**Fig. 1.6** | *Laptop*

### Soak up!

A desktop computer directly runs on electricity. If we turn OFF the power button, the computer will also be turned off. A laptop works on battery which requires electricity to get charged up!

### Today I learned!

- Machines are human-made things. They can perform many tasks easily and quickly.
- A computer is a machine that helps us do many things.
- A computer is a device that takes instructions from the user, stores and processes it, and shows the result.
- A computer has a lot of features that makes it a smart machine.
- A PC or desktop computer is placed on a desk.
- A desktop computer has four parts monitor, CPU, keyboard and mouse.
- A lightweight computer that can be placed on our lap is called a laptop.

# Revise and polish!

**1. Tick (✓) the correct answer.**

a. Tick the machine that can be placed on a desk.

(i) 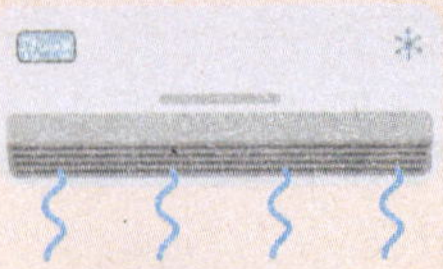 ☐ (ii)  ☐

(iii)  ☐ (iv)  ☐

b. Tick the machine that helps us reach school.

(i)  ☐ (ii)  ☐

(iii) 

☐ (iv)  ☐

c. Tick the object that is not a machine.

(i)  ☐ (ii)  ☐

(iii)  ☐ (iv)  ☐

d. Tick the natural thing.

(i)  ☐ (ii)  ☐

(iii)  ☐ (iv)  ☐

2. **Fill in the blanks using the given words.**

natural human-made laptop many computers

a. All ____________ are machines.

b. A ____________ is a lightweight computer.

c. A computer can perform ____________ tasks.

d. Machines are ____________ things.

e. Trees and mountains are ____________ things.

3. **State whether the following statements are true (T) or false (F).**

a. The mouse on a laptop is called the screen. ☐

b. A computer takes instructions from humans. ☐

c. Machines make our life difficult. ☐

d. A laptop is not a computer. ☐

e. At home, computers are used to play games. ☐

4. **Look at the following pictures. Name the machines being used.**

a.

____________

b.

____________

c.

____________

d.

____________

## 5. Match the following.

| | | | |
|---|---|---|---|
| a. | I can solve complex calculations. | (i) |  |
| b. | I am a natural thing. | (ii) | 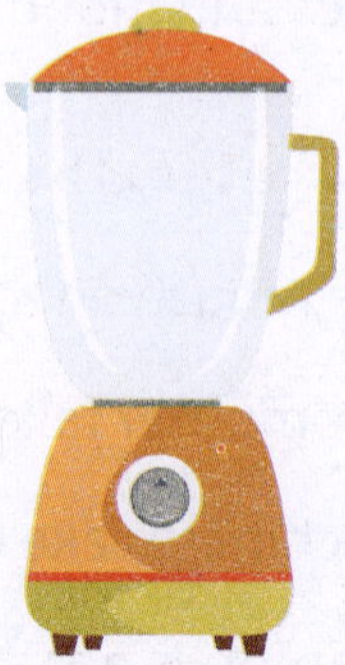 |
| c. | I take you from one place to another. | (iii) |  |
| d. | I can make juice for you. | (iv) |  |
| e. | I help you be on time. | (v) |  |

6. **Join the dots and colour the following pictures.**

a.

b.

## Lab Activity

Visit the computer lab. Do you see any smart machines there? Count and write the number of smart machines you see.

Chapter

2

# Uses of a Computer

**After reading this chapter, I will be able to:**

- ✔ Tell why we use a computer.
- ✔ List the different uses of a computer.
- ✔ Explain the uses of a computer at different places.

## Brainstorm and explore!

Life Skills

**Look at the following pictures. Tick (✔) the activities you can perform with the help of a computer.**

1. Playing in a garden ☐

2. Sending letters/messages to friends ☐

3. Shopping ☐

4. Studying ☐

Computers have become an important part of our daily lives. They make our work easier and faster.

## Reasons for Using a Computer

Some reasons for using a computer are:

1. A computer always gives us correct results.
2. A computer can store a lot of information.
3. A computer never gets tired.
4. A computer remembers everything.
5. A computer can do multiple tasks at the same time.

**Fig. 2.1** | *A Computer*

## Uses of a Computer

A computer is a smart machine. It helps us do many things. Different people use computers for different things. Here are some of the ways in which computers are used:

- We use a computer to learn/look for information on the internet.

**internet**: a global system that connects computers all over the world

**Fig. 2.2** | *To learn/research*

### Clear up!

Look at the following picture. It shows that a computer is a fast machine. Trace the outline to complete the picture. Colour it.

Fig. 2.3 | *Play games*

- We use a computer to play games.

Fig. 2.4 | *Draw and colour pictures*

- We use a computer to draw and colour pictures.

Fig. 2.5 | *Watch movies*

- We use a computer to watch movies.

Fig. 2.6 | *Listen to music*

- We use a computer to listen to music.

Fig. 2.7 | *Talk to people everywhere*

- A computer helps us talk to people far away from us.

- We can send and receive emails using a computer.

**Fig. 2.8** | *Send emails*

- We use a computer to shop online.

**Fig. 2.9** | *Shop online*

**Soak up!**

We can book tickets to a movie show or a sports stadium using a computer.

**Crank up!**

Emails are electronic mails. We can send or receive information using emails. Both the parties should have an email account to send and receive emails.

**Brush up!**

Name some activities that you have done using computers.

______________________________________________

______________________________________________

## Places where Computers are Used

A computer is a smart machine. It is used at different places to do different things.

|  | 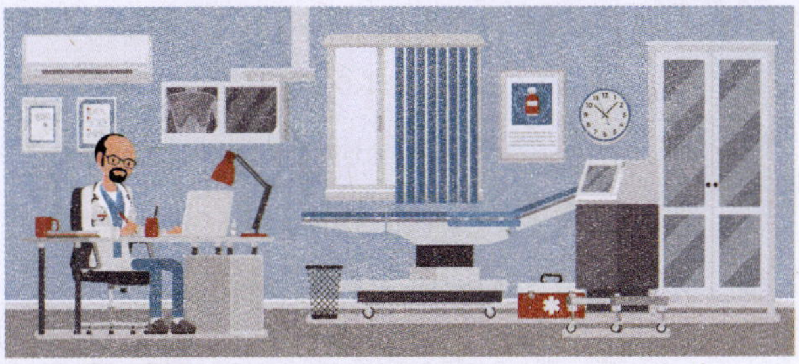 |
|---|---|
| In schools, for teaching and learning | In hospitals, by doctors to maintain their patient records |

| | |
|---|---|
|   |  |
| In banks, to deposit and withdraw money | In offices, to do official work |
|  |  |
| In airports and railway stations, to book tickets and track planes and trains | In labs, by scientists to do research work |

## Clear up!

Can you think of some more places where computers are used?

## Today I learned!

- A computer always gives us correct results.
- A computer can store a lot of information.
- A computer remembers everything and never gets tired.
- A computer can do multiple tasks at the same time.
- A computer is used to learn/research for projects, play games, draw and colour pictures, watch movies, listen to music, talk to people, send emails and shop online.
- We use computers at different places, such as schools, hospitals, banks, offices, railway stations, airports and research labs.

## Revise and polish!

**1. Tick (✓) the correct answer.**

a. Which of the following picture shows that a computer can store a lot of information?

(i)  ☐ (ii)  ☐

(iii)  ☐ (iv)  ☐

b. Which place is used to do research work?

(i)  ☐ (ii)  ☐

(iii) 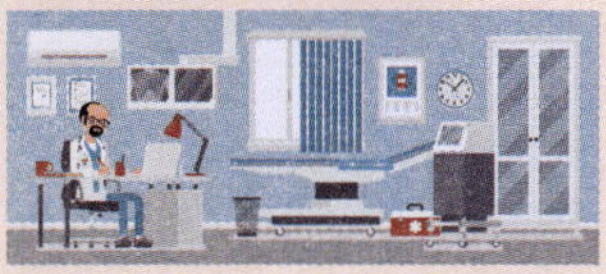 ☐ (iv)  ☐

c. What do you use to send emails?

(i)  ☐ (ii)  ☐

(iii)  ☐ (iv)  ☐

d. Which of these shows use of computers in playing games?

(i)  ☐ (ii)  ☐

(iii)  ☐ (iv)  ☐

e. Which of these features will be used to write a letter to your friend in the UK?

(I) Sending email ☐ (ii) Chatting ☐

(iii) Watching a movie ☐ (iv) Calling ☐

**2. Fill in the blanks using the given words.**

email information music planes talk

a. We can use a computer to listen to ____________.

b. Airports use computers to track ____________.

c. We use a computer to ____________ to our far-off friends.

d. A computer can be used to type an ____________.

e. A computer can store a lot of ____________.

**3. State whether the following statements are true (T) or false (F).**

a. Computers work slower than humans. ☐

b. Computers are used to play in parks. ☐

c. Computers can store a lot of information. ☐

d. Computers are not used in research labs. ☐

e. Computers are used in banks to deposit money. ☐

**4. Search the following words in the word grid given below.**

Music Email Mobile Draw Movie

| | | | | | | | |
|---|---|---|---|---|---|---|---|
| C | M | O | B | I | L | E | R |
| L | E | A | O | Z | S | D | A |
| O | M | O | B | O | T | L | D |
| M | A | J | M | U | S | I | C |
| O | I | D | P | Q | L | F | O |
| V | L | A | N | N | O | T | E |
| I | O | M | E | N | E | C | S |
| E | A | M | E | D | R | A | W |

**5. Colour the activities that you can do using computers.**

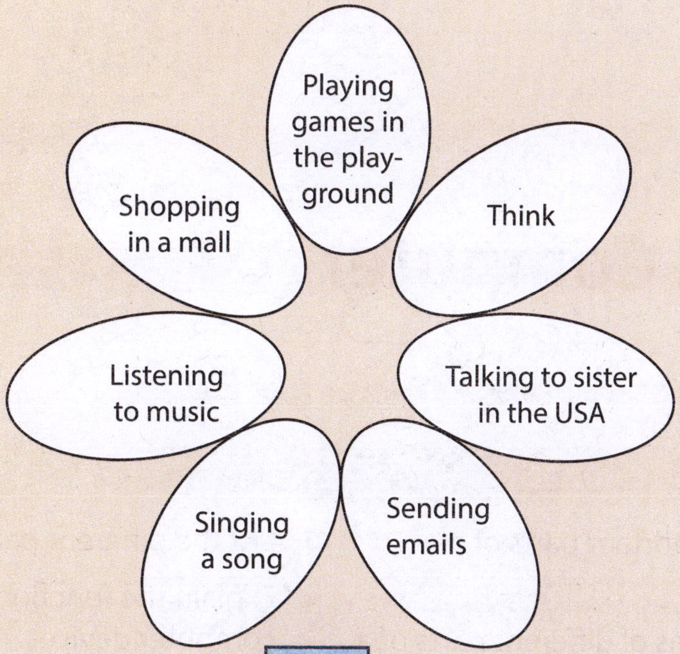


Experiential Learning

## Lab Activity

Computers can be used to type documents, draw pictures or listen to music. In the lab, ask your teacher to show this to you.

Collaboration

## Project

In groups of two, discuss the many uses of computers in your daily lives.

Critical thinking

## Think and Answer

Answer the following questions.

1. Name the last movie you watched on a computer. ______________
2. Which is your favourite song that you like listening to on your computer? ______________
3. When and where did you last use the computer? ______________
4. What is the most used feature of the computer at your home? ______________
5. Which game do you play on the computer/phone? ______________
6. Name the place where you have seen the use of computers the most. ______________
7. Which activity do you do the most on the computer? ______________

Chapter
3

# Parts of a Computer

After reading this chapter, I will be able to:

- ✔ Identify the important parts of a computer.
- ✔ Tell the functions of different parts of a computer.
- ✔ List the different parts of a mouse.
- ✔ Explain the functions of additional computer devices.

## Brainstorm and explore!

**Look at these pictures. Which parts of the body do we use to do these tasks?**

1. Run in the playground

_______________

2. Smell flowers

_______________

3. See things around us

_______________

We have learned in the previous chapters that a *computer is a device that takes instructions from the user, stores and processes it, and shows the result*. Just like humans have different body parts, computers have different parts too. Each part has a function of its own. All the parts work together to make sure the computer runs well.

The four important parts of a computer are:

- Monitor
- CPU
- Keyboard
- Mouse

**Fig. 3.1** | *Parts of a computer*

**Brush up!**

Go to the lab and check if you can point out all the parts of a computer. List the parts here.

______________________________

______________________________

______________________________

______________________________

# Monitor

**Fig. 3.2** | *Monitor*

The monitor looks like a TV screen. It displays the information we give to the computer. It also shows the result. It helps us watch pictures and movies on a computer.

# CPU

CPU stands for **Central Processing Unit**. It is the CPU's job to take instructions from the user and carry them out.

In the human body, the brain does the processing. Hence, the CPU is also known as the **brain of the computer**. The more powerful the CPU, the faster is the computer.

Fig. 3.3 | *CPU*

Technology Literacy

**Crank up!**

All the parts of a computer are connected to the CPU.

# Keyboard

A keyboard is used to give instructions to a computer. It has many buttons called keys. It has letters, numbers, symbols and some special keys.

Fig. 3.4 | *Keyboard*

**Soak up!**

Generally, a keyboard has 101 keys.

**Brush up!**

Look at the keyboard carefully. Why is it called QWERTY keyboard?

**Hint:** Check the third row on your keyboard.

___

___

# Mouse

Fig. 3.5 | *Computer mouse*

A mouse is used to point at different things on the monitor. It is used to give inputs to the computer. We can use the mouse to take the cursor to different parts of the screen and click on icons.

The mouse is also used for selecting, dragging, clicking and opening programs or games.

**cursor**: the moving pointer on the computer that points to the position of the mouse

## Parts of a Mouse

A mouse has four main parts, as shown in Fig. 3.6.

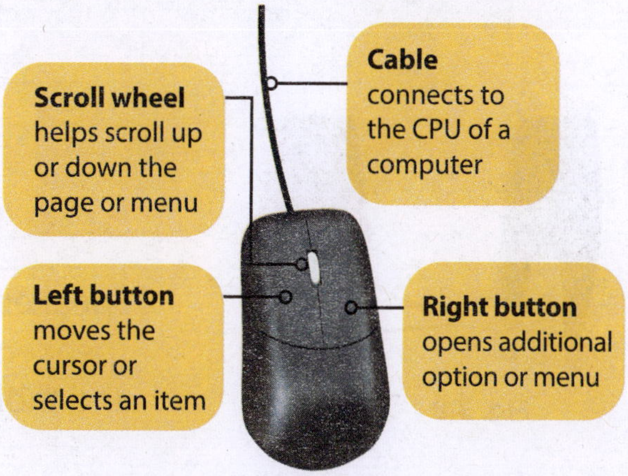


Fig. 3.6 | *Parts of a computer mouse*

1. **Left or primary button**: A mouse has two buttons on it. The left button is used to move the cursor or select an item on the computer screen.
2. **Right or secondary button**: The right button is used to get an additional option or menu for a specific item.
3. **Scroll wheel**: The scroll wheel is always in the centre of the mouse. It helps us scroll up and down a page.
4. **Cable**: The cable connects the mouse to the CPU of a computer. Today, many computer mice are available to be used without a wire as well (wireless mouse).

**Soak up!**

A gaming mouse can have 4 or 5 buttons.

**Crank up!** Technology Literacy

Laptops have touchpads that can be used to point on the monitor. That is why, laptops do not need a mouse. Similarly, the CPU is situated inside the laptop, and thus, we cannot see it from the outside.

We have read about the monitor, CPU, keyboard and the mouse. There are other devices that can be connected to the computer for various purposes. Let us learn about these.

## Printer

A printer is used to take printouts on a piece of paper. It can print pictures and letters.

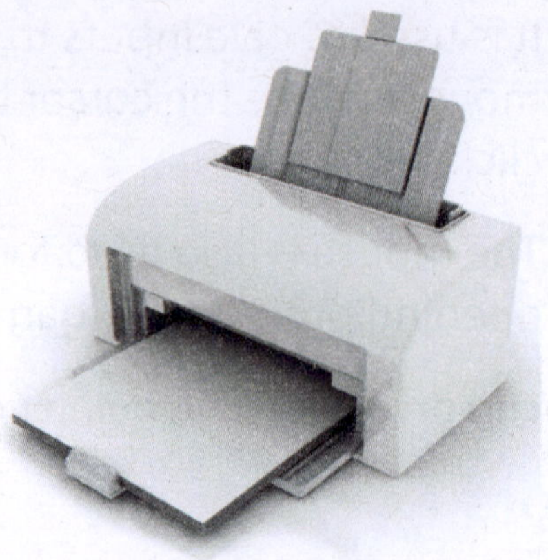

**Fig. 3.7** | *Printer*

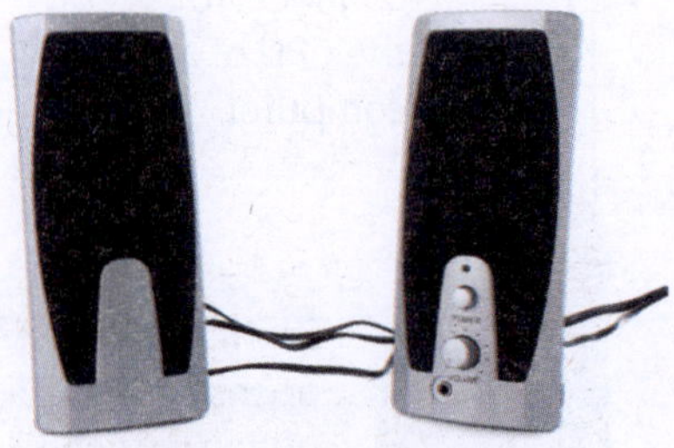

**Fig. 3.8** | *Speakers*

## Speakers

Speakers enable the computer to play sound. We use speakers to listen to songs and watch movies. Laptops and tablets have in-built speakers in them.

**tablet**: a small flat computer that you operate by touching the screen

## Webcam

A webcam is used to make video calls and take pictures. Laptops and tablets have in-built cameras. Most desktop monitors do not have an in-built camera and require a separate webcam.

**Fig. 3.9** | *Webcam*

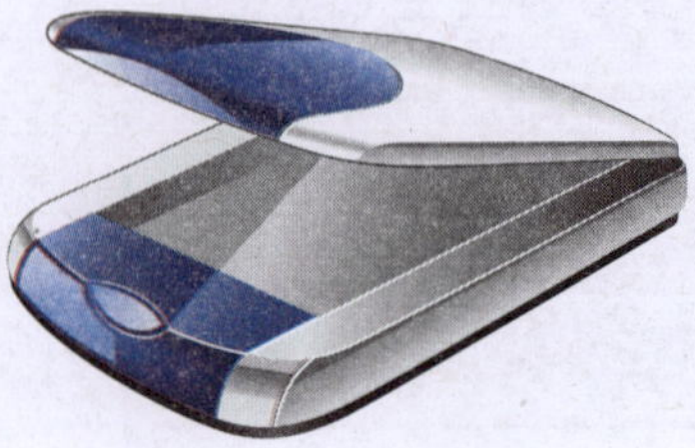

**Fig. 3.10** | *Scanner*

## Scanner

A scanner is used to scan pictures of physical documents and images. These pictures can be transferred to a computer.

## Clear up!

Name the parts of a computer.

1. 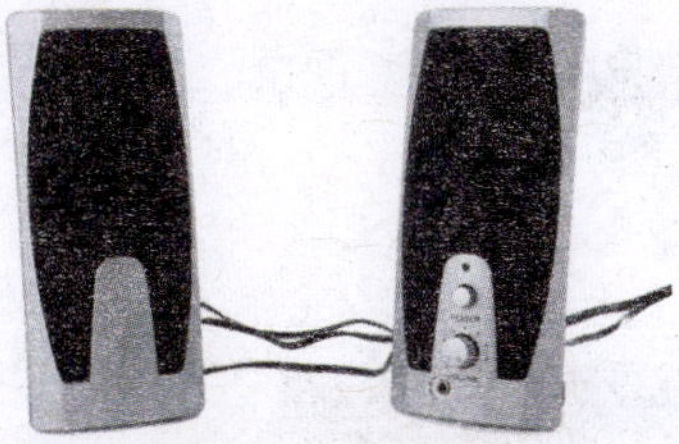

2. 

3. 

4. 

5. 

6. 

## Today I learned!

- The main parts of a computer are the monitor, CPU, keyboard and mouse.
- A monitor is also known as the screen. It displays information or results back to the user.
- The CPU is the brain of the computer. It helps run and process everything on the computer.
- A keyboard is used to give instructions to a computer. It has many buttons called keys.
- A mouse is used to give inputs to the computer. It is used to move the cursor or select an item on the screen.
- A mouse has four basic parts—left and right buttons, scroll wheel and a cable.
- A printer is used to print pictures and letters on a piece of paper.
- Speakers enable the computer to play sound.
- A webcam is used to make video calls and take pictures.
- A scanner is used to scan pictures of physical documents and images. It can also transfer them on the computer screen.

## Revise and polish!

**1. Tick (✓) the correct answer.**

a. Select the device used to select an item on the screen.

(i)  ☐ (ii)  ☐

(iii)  ☐ (iv)  ☐

b. Which device is used to take printouts?

(i)  ☐ (ii) 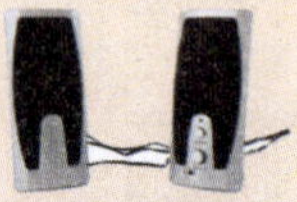 ☐

(iii)  ☐ (iv) 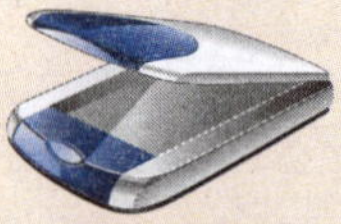 ☐

c. Tick the device used to listen to songs.

(i) 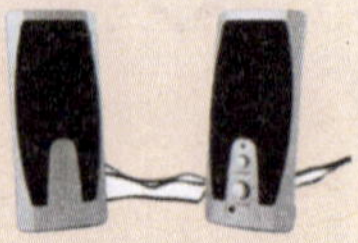 ☐ (ii)  ☐

(iii)  ☐ (iv)  ☐

d. Tick the device that looks like a monitor.

(i)  ☐ (ii)  ☐

(iii)  ☐ (iv)  ☐

e. Tick the device used to copy the image of a physical document to the computer.

(i)  ☐ (ii)  ☐

(iii)  ☐ (iv)  ☐

**2. Fill in the blanks using the given words.**

webcam  symbols  tablets  two  CPU

a. The ____________ is known as the brain of the computer.

b. The mouse has ____________ buttons and a scroll wheel.

c. The keyboard contains letters, numbers, ____________ and special keys.

d. The ____________ is used to make video calls and take pictures.

e. Laptops and ____________ have inbuilt speakers in them.

**3. State whether the following statements are true (T) or false (F).**

a. The monitor looks like a TV screen.

b. A wireless mouse has a long cable.

c. A printer can print pictures and letters.

d. Desktop monitors have an in-built keyboard.

e. Buttons on the mouse are called keys.

**4. Match the following.**

| | | | |
|---|---|---|---|
| a. | Brain of the computer | (i) |  |
| b. | Used to type a letter | (ii) |  |
| c. | Displays output to the user | (iii) | 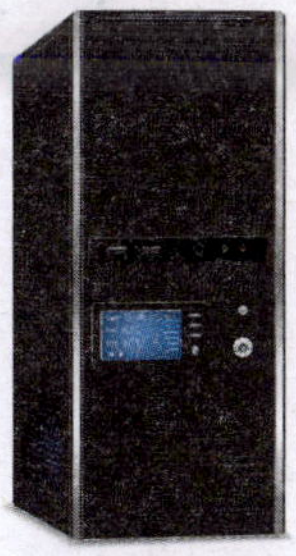 |
| d. | A mouse without a wire | (iv) |  |
| e. | Used to make video calls | (v) |  |

5. **Name the parts of the computer used to do the following tasks.**

a. Watching movies: _________

b. Make video calls: _________

c. Taking printouts: _________

d. Typing: _________

6. **You already know about various parts of a computer system. Now, mark the following parts on the given picture of a laptop.**

Monitor Touchpad Keyboard

Experiential Learning

## Lab Activities

1. Monitor, mouse, keyboard, speakers, etc., are connected to the CPU with the help of wires. In the computer lab, ask the teacher to show this to you.
2. Try using the mouse by clicking on the right and left buttons. Use the scroll wheel to go up and down the page.
3. In the computer lab, see how to use the following devices with the help of your teacher.
   a. How to type using the keyboard?
   b. How to turn the monitor ON and OFF or use it to play videos?
   c. How to switch on the computer using the CPU?
   d. How to use the mouse to open a document?
   e. How to print the document on a school computer?

Collaboration

## Group Activities

1. Go through all the keys in the keyboard and discuss what each of them do with your classmates.
2. Form groups of 10 and participate in role-play activities to identify and state the functions of the main parts of the computer. Each group can assign a few members as one part of the computer. You can wear cutouts made of cardboard or paper and dress up as that part. Describe the use of that particular part to the rest of the class.

Chapter 4

# Using Computers—Dos and Don'ts

**After reading this chapter, I will be able to:**

- ✔ Discuss the importance of using machines properly.
- ✔ Implement the safety rules while using a computer.
- ✔ Maintain the correct posture while using a computer.
- ✔ Understand taking care of computers in school and at home.

Life Skills

## Brainstorm and explore!

**Look at the following pictures. What will happen if you handle them without care or do not store them properly?**

1. Bicycle

2. Pieces of a board game

A computer has many parts. It is important for all the parts to work together properly. Therefore, we should take good care of them.

# Safety Rules

A computer runs on electricity. The CPU and the monitor are connected to power supply. All other parts of the computer are connected to the CPU with wires. We should take care of these points while turning a computer on:

- Make sure the switch is off before inserting the power plug.
- Do not touch the wires that connect different parts of a computer. Sometimes, they may carry electrical charge.
- After using the computer, always shut it down. Before removing the power plug, make sure the switch is off.
- Always use a computer in the presence of elders.

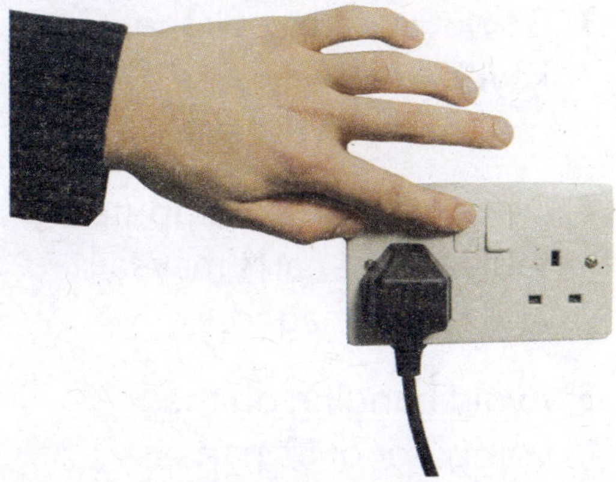

**Fig. 4.1** | *Switchboard*

**Clear up!**

Discuss in the class how a laptop gets its power. Also, discuss how we can maintain safety precautions with laptops.

# Using the Computer

Computer is a smart machine. It helps us perform many tasks. While using a computer, we need to take care of it as well as of ourselves.

## Handling the Computer

While using a computer, we must take care of the following points:

### Keeping the Computer Clean

- Always use a dry cloth or brush to wipe the computer.
- Keep the computer room clean. Dust can damage the computer.
- Do not eat or drink anything while using the computer. Food or drinks may spill on it.

**Fig. 4.2** | *Cleaning a computer*

## Using the Computer

- Do not push or pull the keyboard and mouse. It may damage the wires.
- Do not push the computer table. Some parts may fall and get damaged.
- Avoid banging on the computer or its parts.

Fig. 4.3 | *Using a computer properly*

While using a shared computer with a family member or a classmate, ensure the following:

- Take turns while using the computer so that everyone gets a chance.
- Keep the volume low so that others do not get disturbed.

Fig. 4.4 | *Using a shared computer*

## Maintaining Correct Posture

What will happen if you keep your hand up in the air for more than 10 minutes?

Our body parts ache if we do not use them in the right manner or over-stretch them. Similarly, while working on a computer, it is important to maintain the correct posture.

**posture**: the position of the different parts of the body while sitting, walking and standing

**Fig. 4.5** | *Correct posture while using a computer*

One should take care of the following points to maintain correct posture:

- Use a comfortable chair. Make sure the chair is adjusted to the height of the monitor.
- Your chin should not point up or down. It should be facing the monitor straight.
- Your back should be straight.
- Rest your hand comfortably on the table while typing.
- The monitor should not be too close or too far away from the eyes. This will reduce the strain on the eyes.

## Clear up!

In addition to computers and laptops, smartphones are widely used today. Look at the following pictures. Tick (✓) the correct postures and cross (✗) the incorrect postures.

1. a.  ☐

b.  ☐

2. a.  ☐

b.  ☐

3. a.  ☐

b.  ☐

## Today I learned!

- Computers help us perform a wide range of tasks. We must use a computer carefully and gently.
- We should turn off the power button while inserting and removing the power plug.
- We should not touch the wires of computer parts.
- We should always shut down a computer after use.
- We should use a computer in the presence of elders.
- We should always keep the computer room clean.
- We should share the computer resources for everyone's use.
- It is important to be mindful of one's posture while using the computer or a laptop.

## Revise and polish!

Learning Skills

**1. Tick (✓) the correct answer.**

a. All the computer parts have wires connected to the ____________.

(i) monitor ☐ (ii) CPU ☐

(iii) keyboard ☐ (iv) mouse ☐

b. After using the computer, always ____________ it down.

(i) lock ☐ (ii) put ☐ (iii) restart ☐ (iv) shut ☐

c. Which of these should be used to wipe a computer?

(i) A wet cloth ☐ (ii) A dry cloth ☐

(iii) A dirty cloth ☐ (iv) A paper ☐

d. Which of these practices should be followed while using a shared computer?

(i) Eating on the table ☐ (ii) Not cleaning the computer ☐

(iii) Listening to loud music ☐ (iv) Taking turns to use a computer ☐

e. While working on a computer, it is important to ____________.

(i) maintain the correct posture ☐ (ii) lean on the desk ☐

(iii) sit too close to the screen ☐ (iv) keep a hand on the chair ☐

**2. Fill in the blanks using the given words.**

monitor songs posture dry electricity

a. A computer runs on ____________.

b. We should maintain the correct ____________ while using a computer.

c. We should use a ____________ cloth to wipe the computer.

d. It is important to keep the ____________ at the right distance from the eyes.

e. Keep the volume low while playing ____________ on the computer.

**3. Match the following.**

| | | | |
|---|---|---|---|
| a. | Before inserting the power plug | (i) | Wipe your computer |
| b. | Use a dry cloth to | (ii) | Keep your back straight |
| c. | Keep the volume low | (iii) | Make sure the switch is OFF |
| d. | While using a computer | (iv) | To not disturb others |

**4. Look at the following pictures. Tick (✓) the dos and cross (✗) the don'ts.**

a.

☐

b.

☐

c.

☐

d.

☐

e.

☐

f.

☐

**5. Number the following steps in the correct order.**

| Turn the switch ON. | Insert the plug. | Make sure the switch is OFF. |
|---|---|---|
| ☐ | ☐ | ☐ |

**6. Answer the following questions.**

| Dos while using a computer | Don'ts while using a computer |
|---|---|
| a. | d. |
| b. | e. |
| c. | f. |

## Lab Activities

1. Practice all the dos and don'ts while using a computer in the lab.
2. While exiting the computer lab, ensure the classmate next to you has switched off the computer properly. All students should look at the next classmate's computer to check if it has been shut down properly.

## Group Activities

We have learned about the dos and don'ts of using computers. In groups of three, discuss the dos and don'ts for the following devices:

a. Smartphone

b. Television

Chapter 5

# Computer Keyboard

**After reading this chapter, I will be able to:**

- ✔ Identify the different keys on a keyboard.
- ✔ Use the main typing keys and navigation keys on a keyboard.
- ✔ Identify and locate the numeric keypad and the function keys on a keyboard.

Learning Skills

## Brainstorm and explore!

**Think and write the names of five activities for which you use the keyboard specifically. One has been done for you.**

1. I use the keyboard to **play games.**
2. I use the keyboard to______________________________.
3. I use the keyboard to ______________________________.
4. I use the keyboard to ______________________________.

A keyboard is used to enter information into a computer. Without it, sending any information into the computer is difficult. There are different types of keyboards. The QWERTY keyboard is used most commonly.

**Soak up!**

In the QWERTY keyboard, the letters Q, W, E, R, T and Y come together in the first row. Hence, the name QWERTY.

# Keys on a Keyboard

A keyboard has 101 keys that can be divided into four major groups based on their uses. This is shown in Fig. 5.1.

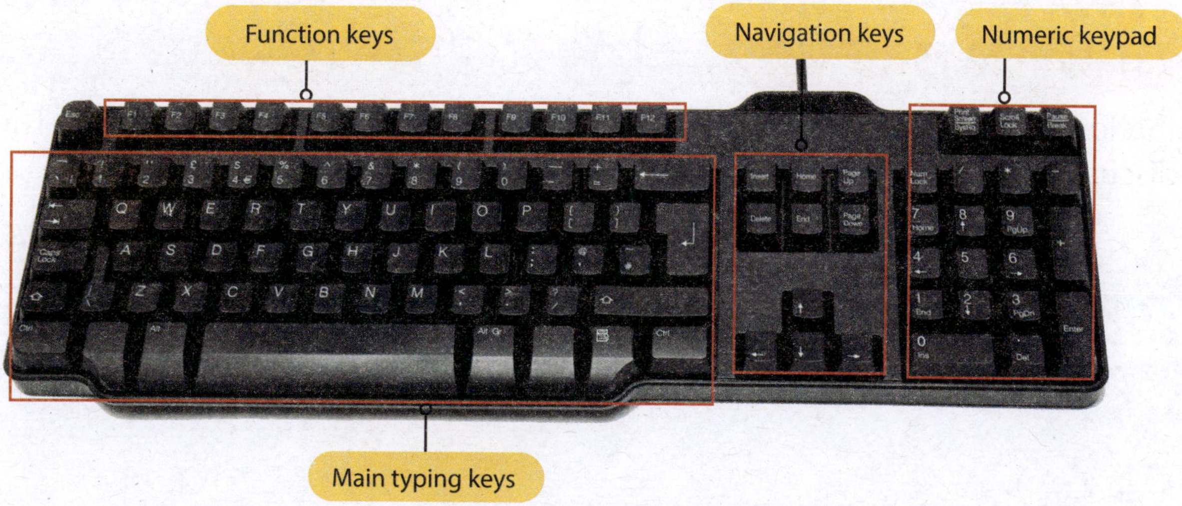


**Fig. 5.1** | *Keys on a keyboard*

## Main Typing Keys

The main typing keypad on a keyboard consists of **alphabet keys** (keys from A–Z), **number keys** (keys from 0–9), **special keys** and **control keys**.

1. Alphabet keys are the letters from A-Z. They can be used to type small or capital letters. There are a total 26 letters on the keyboard.
2. Number keys are present on the top row of the keyboard. These keys are numbers from 0 to 9.
3. In addition to letters, numbers, punctuation marks ( ., ;, :, "), and symbols (+, –, *, &, %), the typing keys also include special keys. These special keys are Shift, Caps Lock, Tab, Enter, Spacebar and Backspace.
   - The *Spacebar* key moves the cursor one space forward.
   - The *Enter* key moves the cursor to the next line.
   - The *Caps Lock* key is used to switch between capital and small letters. When the Caps Lock key is ON, we can type capital letters. The *Shift* key is also used for the same reason. However, the *Shift* key has to be used along with other keys.

**Crank up!**

The small LED light on top of the Caps Lock key shows that the Caps Lock button is ON.

4. Control keys are the keys used to perform special actions. The most frequently used control keys are Ctrl, Alt, Windows logo key and Esc. Mostly, there are two Ctrl and two Alt keys on the keyboard, located on the left and right side of the last row of the keyboard.

## Navigation Keys

Navigation keys are used for moving around in a document or playing a game. These are discussed in Table 5.1.

**Table 5.1** *Navigation keys*

| Keys | Function of the key |
|---|---|
| **Arrow keys**   | Arrow keys are used to move the cursor up, down, left and right. |
| **Home and End keys** 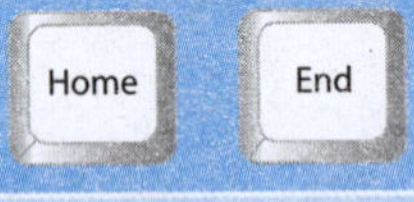  | Home key is used to go to the beginning of a line, while End key is used to move to the end of a line. |
| **Page Up and Page Down keys** 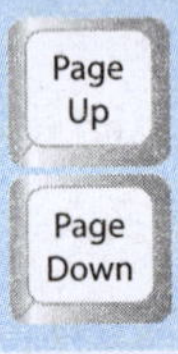  | Page Up and Page Down keys are used to scroll through the screen one page at a time. |
| **Delete key**   | Delete key is used to delete/erase text. This can be done by either selecting the text and pressing delete or by deleting letter by letter. |
| **Insert key**   | Insert key can be used to turn the insert mode OFF or ON. This is used to insert text or image while typing. |

**Brush up!**

Which of these keys are most widely used?

1. Navigation keys ☐  2. Main typing keys ☐  3. Control keys ☐

## Numeric Keypad

To use this keypad, we should turn on the **Num Lock** key. The numeric keypad consists of numbers, navigation keys (Delete, Home, Page up, Page down, Insert, Enter), as well as mathematical operators, such as addition (+), subtraction (–), multiplication (*) and division (/).

**Fig. 5.2** | *Numeric keypad*

**Soak up!**

The numeric keypad is not found on all keyboards. For example, keyboards on laptops, tablets and phones do not have a numeric keypad.

## Function Keys

Function keys are used to perform specific tasks. They are placed on the top row of the keyboard and are labelled as F1, F2, F3, and so on, up to F12. The uses of these keys depends on the program. For example, the F1 key is used to open the Help menu.

**Clear up!**

Rearrange the jumbled letters. Write their correct names in the space given.

1. SERTIN ________________
2. FISHT ________________
3. MOHE ________________
4. LKCCPOSA ________________

**Today I learned!**

- A keyboard has 101 keys that can be divided into 4 major groups.
- Alphabet keys are used to type letters from A to Z.
- Number keys are used to type numbers from 0 to 9.
- Capslock is used to switch between capital and small letters.
- Spacebar is used to move the cursor forward.
- Control keys are the keys used to perform special actions. The most frequently used control keys are Ctrl, Alt, the Windows logo key and Esc.
- Navigation keys are used for moving around in documents.
- The Numeric keypad consists of numbers, navigation keys and mathematical operators.
- The function keys (F1-F12) are used to perform specific tasks.

## Revise and polish!

**1. Tick (✓) the correct answer.**

a. Which one of these is not a navigation key?

(i) Delete ☐ (ii) Page Up ☐

(iii) Spacebar ☐ (iv) Enter ☐

b. Which one of these is a part of the main typing keys?

(i) Page Up ☐ (ii) Home ☐

(iii) Spacebar ☐ (iv) Num Lock ☐

c. Which of these is used to insert text or image while typing?

(i) Clt ☐ (ii) Alt ☐ (iii) Insert ☐ (iv) Page Down ☐

d. Which key is used to move the cursor to the next line?

(i) Spacebar ☐ (ii) Enter ☐ (iii) Tab ☐ (iv) Caps Lock ☐

e. Which of the following keys is used to switch from small letters to capital letters while typing?

(i) Caps Lock ☐ (ii) Tab ☐ (iii) Enter ☐ (iv) Insert ☐

**2. Fill in the blanks using the given words.**

F1 arrow key up Num Lock Spacebar Page Up

a. The ____________ key is used to move the cursor up.

b. To turn the Numeric keypad ON, press the ____________ key.

c. The ____________ key is used to open the Help menu.

d. To move the page up, press the ____________ key.

e. Press the ____________ key to move the cursor one space forward.

3. **State whether the following statements are true (T) or false (F).**

a. Special keys are used to type numbers and letters. [ ]

b. The Enter key moves the cursor to the next line. [ ]

c. Home key is used to insert text or image while typing. [ ]

d. Navigation keys are used for moving around in the documents. [ ]

e. We can use the numeric keypad to solve sums on a computer. [ ]

4. **Match the following.**

| | | | |
|---|---|---|---|
| a. | F12 | (i) | Navigation key |
| b. | Page Up | (ii) | Function key |
| c. | Enter | (iii) | Control key |
| d. | Alt | (iv) | Main typing key |
| e. | Num Lock | (v) | Numeric keypad |

5. **Label the following keys on a keyboard:**

a. ____________ b. ____________ c. ____________

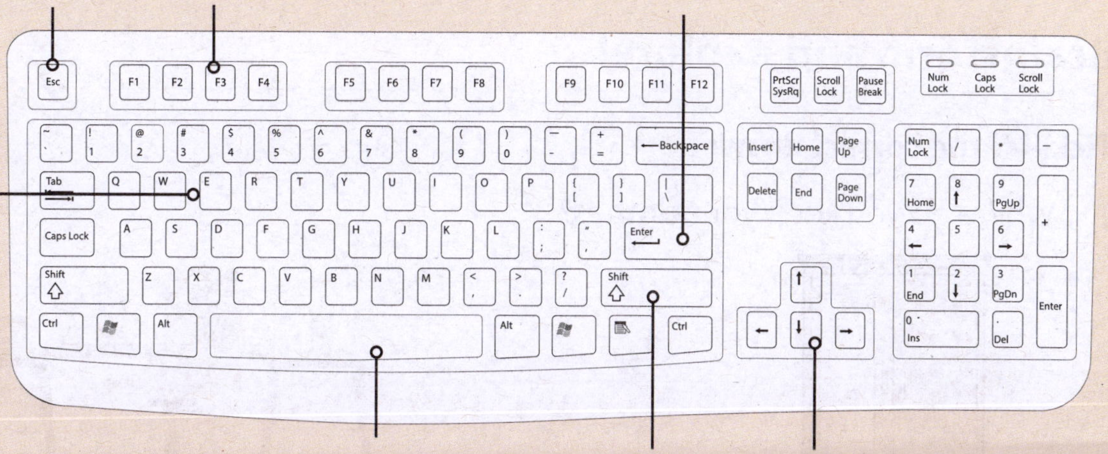

d. ____________ e. ____________ f. ____________ g. ____________

## Lab Activities

Experiential Learning

1. Have you noticed every keyboard in the lab is connected to the computer? Where on the computer is the other side of the wire connected to? ____________

2. Check out with your teacher what each and every key on a computer does and name the keys used to:
   a. Go to the next line in a document: ____________
   b. Type capital letters: ____________
   c. Type the plus sign: ____________
   d. Erase text: ____________

Chapter

6

# Storage Devices

**After reading this chapter, I will be able to:**

- ✔ What are storage devices?
- ✔ What are different storage devices?
- ✔ What is the need for storage devices?

## Brainstorm and explore!

Life Skills

**Tick (✔) the correct answer.**

1. Where do you keep your clothes?

a.

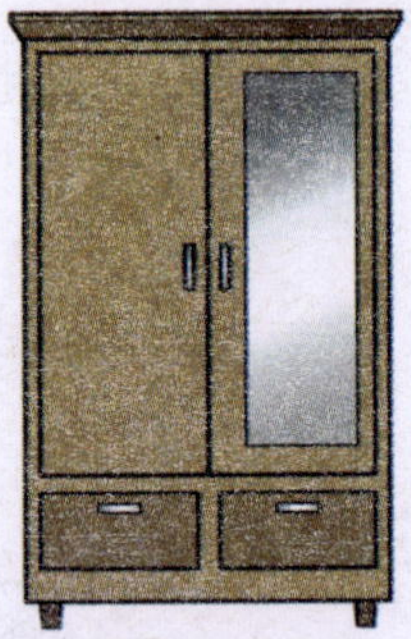

☐

b.

☐

2. Where do you get ice creams from?

a.

☐

b.

☐

We use a bag to store our textbooks, notebooks, pencil box and water bottle. Without it, we will lose most of our items. Similarly, there are devices used to store data in the computer. These are called **storage devices**. Storage devices can be internal or external to the computer. They can be used to store data permanently or temporarily.

Storage devices are used to store information in the computer either permanently or temporarily.

**data**: type of information stored in a computer

**internal**: placed inside the computer

**external**: placed outside the computer

# Different Types of Storage Devices

Let us learn about different types of storage devices.

## Hard Disk

This is the most common type of storage device. Hard drives or hard disks are used to store large amounts of data. There are two types of hard disks:

**Internal Hard Disks**: They are stored inside the CPU. They store applications and files that are easily accessible for the users of the computer.

**External Hard Disks**: They are present as separate devices to store information.

**Fig. 6.1** | *Internal hard disk*

**Fig. 6.2** | *External hard disk*

## CD/DVD

A CD or a DVD is a circular disc that can store a lot of information. A computer can read from a CD or a DVD using the CD/DVD drive. A DVD can store more information than a CD.

**Fig. 6.3** | *A CD and a CD/DVD drive*

**Soak up!**

The full form of CD is Compact Disc and the full form of DVD is Digital Versatile Disc.

## Pen Drive

A pen drive is used to transfer data from one computer to another. It is also known as **flash drive**. A pen drive is very small. You can carry it in your pocket.

**Fig. 6.4** | *Pen drive*

**Fig. 6.5** | *Memory card*

## Memory Card

A memory card is mostly used in phones and cameras to store documents, pictures and videos. It is also known as SD (Secure Digital) memory card.

## Floppy Disk

Floppy disks are thin disks with a square plastic covering. Over the years, they have been made into different shapes and sizes. A floppy disk can store a very small amount of data. Thus, it is no longer used.

**Fig. 6.6** | *Floppy disk*

# Need for Storage Devices

A computer uses storage devices to store all types of information/data (text, images, videos and files downloaded from the internet) for any amount of time. A computer needs storage devices for the following reasons:

- Storage devices make it possible to access the stored files anytime.
- These devices are used to back up important files or data.
- Storage devices make it possible for users to free up computer memory.
- External storage devices make it easier to share and transfer data.

**Soak up!**

We always do not need a physical device to store data. We can store large amounts of data over the internet. This data can be accessed from anywhere and at anytime. This is called cloud storage.

## Brush up!

Rearrange the jumbled letters. Write their correct names in the space given.

1. RDHA KSDI 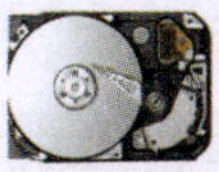 ____________
2. NEP IREVD  ____________
3. VDD 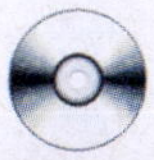 ____________
4. PPYFLO SKDI  ____________

## Crank up!

Technology Literacy

The evolution of storage devices took place in the following order:

Floppy disk → Hard drive → CD → DVD → Pen drive → Memory card → Cloud storage

## Today I learned!

- Storage devices are the devices used to store information in the computer either permanently or temporarily.
- Hard drives or hard disks are used to store large amounts of data.
- If data is stored inside the CPU, it is called an internal hard disk. If it is present as a separate storage device, it is called an external hard disk.
- A CD or a DVD is a circular disc that can store a lot of information.
- A pen drive is used to transfer data from one computer to another.
- A memory card is used in phones and cameras to store documents, pictures and videos.
- A floppy disk can store very small amounts of data.
- A computer uses storage devices, as they store all types of files for any amount of time to be accessed later.
- Storage devices can be internal or external.

## Revise and polish!

**1. Tick (✓) the correct answer.**

a. Which of these devices are used to store data in computers?

(i) Output devices ☐ (ii) Input/Output ☐

(iii) Input devices ☐ (iv) Storage devices ☐

b. A DVD can store more information than a ______.

(i) CD ☐ (ii) External hard disk ☐

(iii) Internal hard disk ☐ (iv) CD drive ☐

c. A pen drive is also known as a ________ drive.

(i) optical ☐ (ii) flash ☐

(iii) magnetic ☐ (iv) disk ☐

d. Which of these storage devices in no longer used?

(i) Hard disk ☐ (ii) Pen drive ☐

(iii) Memory card ☐ (iv) Floppy disk ☐

e. Which of these sentences is wrong about the storage devices?

(i) These devices are used to back up important files or data. ☐

(ii) These devices make it possible to access the stored files anytime, anywhere. ☐

(iii) Internal storage devices make it easier to carry data from one place to another. ☐

(iv) Some storage devices do not require a power supply. ☐

**2. Fill in the blanks using the given words.**

hard disk   images   external   storage   memory card

a. Storage devices can be internal or ____________.

b. An internal ____________ can be stored inside the CPU.

c. A ____________ is also known as SD card.

d. Devices used to store data are called ____________ devices.

e. A computer uses storage devices to store files, such as ____________, text and videos.

**3. State whether the following statements are true (T) or false (F).**

a. Floppy disks are used to store large amount of data. ☐

b. Storage devices can be internal or external. ☐

c. A pen drive cannot be carried from one place to another. ☐

d. A DVD is a rectangular disc that can store a lot of information. ☐

e. Storage devices are used to back up important files or data. ☐

**4. Match the following.**

| | | | |
|---|---|---|---|
| a. | One of the oldest external storage devices. | (i) |  |
| b. | Used to store data internally. | (ii) |  |
| c. | Used to store data externally. | (iii) |  |
| d. | Used to store data in mobile phones. | (iv) |  |
| e. | Used to read data from CD/DVD. | (v) |  |

5. **Complete the crossword with the help of the picture clues.**

6. **Colour the following devices using your favourite colours.**

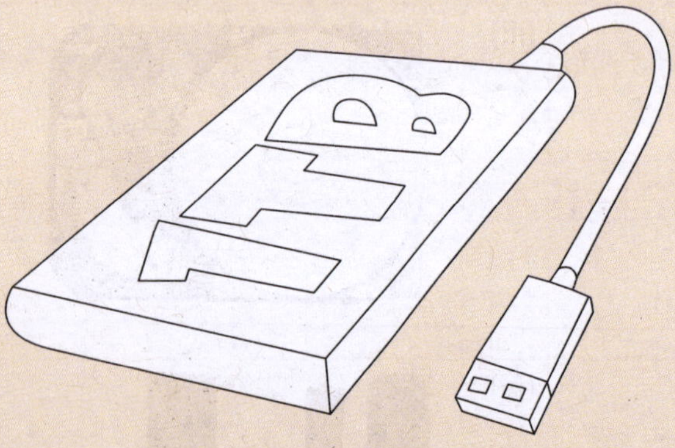


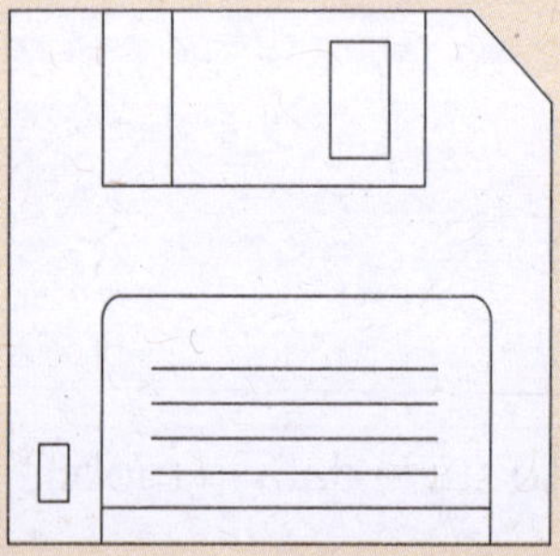

Experiential Learning

## Lab Activities

1. In the lab, ask your teacher to show you some storage devices.
2. Make a list of the storage capacities of different devices available in the lab.

# Worksheet 1 (Chapters 1 and 2)

Technology Literacy

Art Integration

**1. Answer the following questions in one word.**

a. Name the place where a computer is used for students to study. __________

b. Name the place where a computer is used to deposit money. __________

c. Name an activity for which you use a computer. __________

d. Which machine do you use the most? __________

e. Name any one machine you have in your study room. __________

f. Name the place where your dad uses a computer. __________

**2. Colour the pictures of machines.**

| a. | 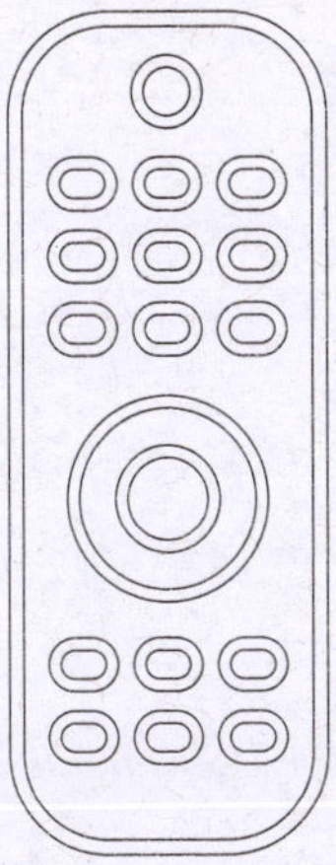 | b. | 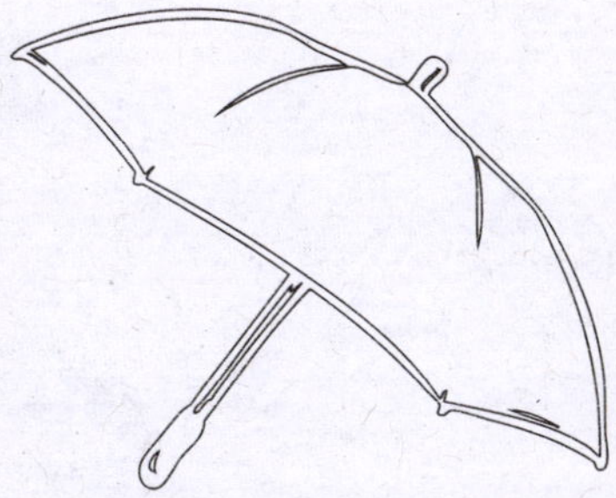 | c. | 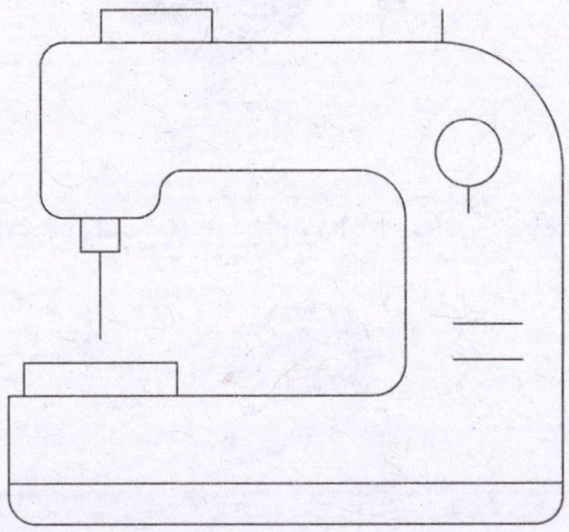 |
|---|---|---|---|---|---|
| d. | 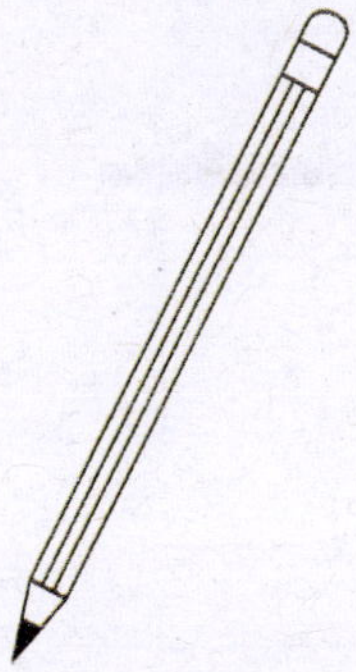 | e. |  | f. |  |

# Worksheet 2 (Chapters 3 and 4)

**1. Fill in the blanks using the correct word.**

a. A ____________ (keyboard/mouse) is used to move the cursor on the screen.

b. Always use a ____________ (wet/dry) cloth or brush to wipe the computer.

c. All the computer parts have wires connected to the ____________ (CPU/mouse).

d. The ____________ (monitor/scanner) looks like a TV screen.

e. It is not ____________ (safe/unsafe) to touch the wires of computer parts.

**2. Tick (✔) the correct answer.**

a. Which of these parts of a computer are used to make video calls?

(i)  ☐ (ii)  ☐

b. Select the right way to hold a mouse.

(i)  ☐ (ii)  ☐

c. Select the right way to sit in front of a computer.

(i)  ☐ (ii)  ☐

d. Tick the part of computer you will use to type a document.

(i)  ☐ (ii) 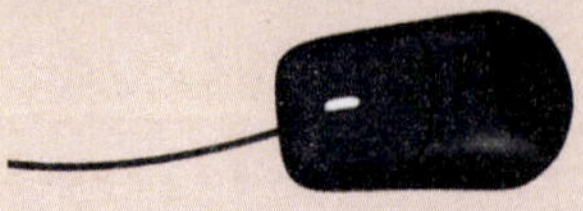 ☐

3. **Draw a computer mouse by tracing your hand. What other computer parts can you draw by tracing your hand?**

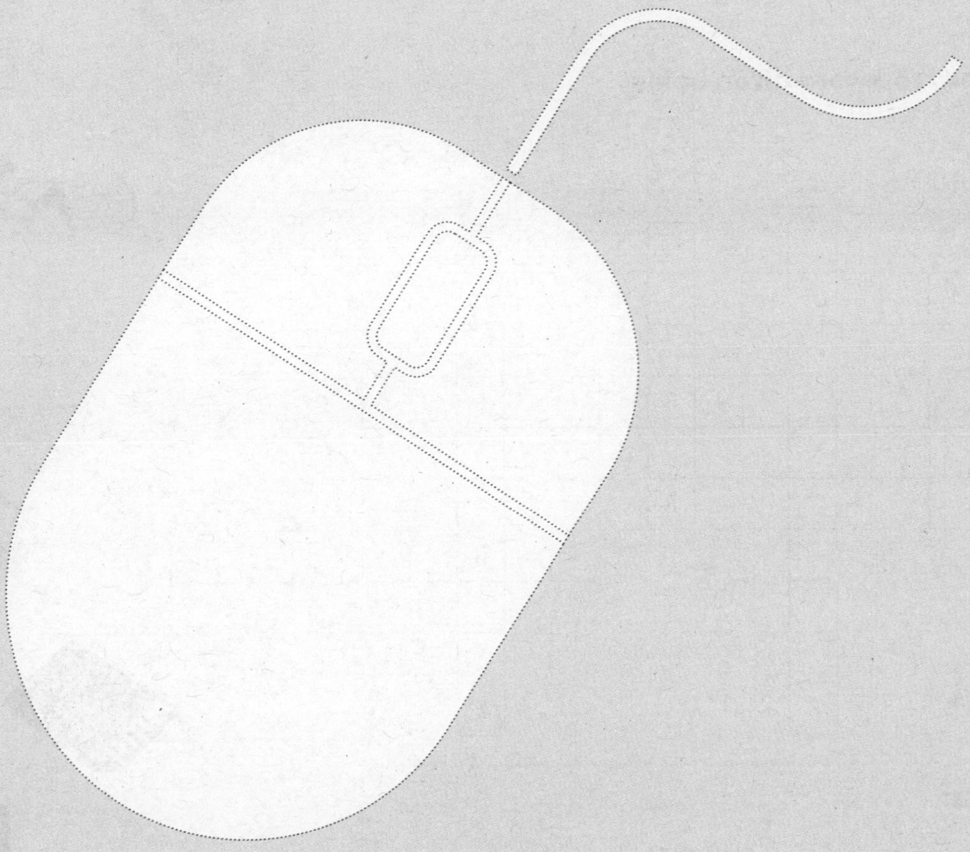

# Worksheet 3 (Chapters 5 and 6)

Problem-solving | Technology Literacy

**1. Solve the crossword given below.**

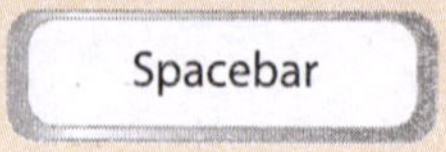

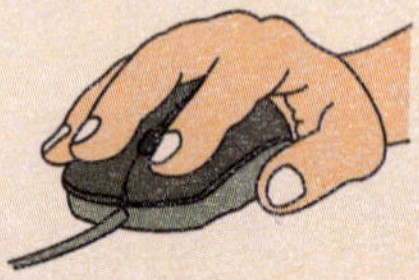

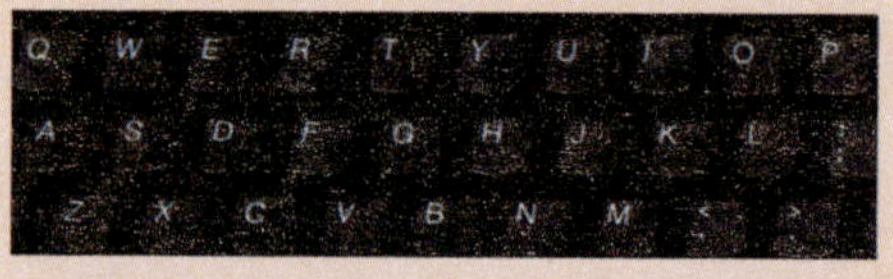

**Across:**

3. Connects a mouse to the CPU
5. Letters from A-Z
6. Mostly used in phones and cameras
7. Move the cursor up, down, left and right

**Down:**

1. Moves the cursor forward
2. A thin disk with a square plastic covering
4. A portable storage device

**2. Who am I?**

a. I help you switch between capital and small letters. ____________

b. I am a device used to transfer pictures from one laptop to another. ____________

c. I am used for moving around in documents. ____________

d. I am a storage device used in cameras. ____________

e. I am a key used to move to the next line. ____________

## Additional Worksheet

**1. Fill in the missing terms. One has been done for you.**

| | | | | |
|---|---|---|---|---|
| a. | A | B | C | D |
| b. | 1 | | | 4 |
| c. | | X | | Z |
| d. | | | 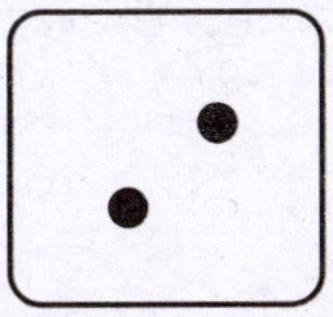 | 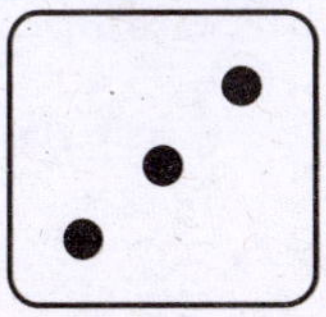 |

**2. Add the numbers and complete the following table. Colour your answer.**

1

1 + 1 = 2

1 + 1 + 1 = ☐

1 + 1 + 1 + 1 = ☐

1 + 1 + 1 + 1 + 1 = ☐

Do you see something common in the coloured boxes? Can you guess what is it?

______________________________

**3. Identify the following shapes in the images given. Name the object(s) in the image that have the shape.**

| Circle | Triangle |
|---|---|
| <br>a. ______________________ | <br>b. ______________________ |
| Rectangle | Oval |
| <br>c. ______________________ | <br>d. ______________________ |

Using these shapes, create a new drawing.

## Fun Activity

**Follow the given path and lead the rabbit to the carrot.**

CLASS 1

QUESTION PAPER SET A

# NCO

SOF NATIONAL CYBER OLYMPIAD 2021-22

DO NOT OPEN THIS BOOKLET UNTIL ASKED TO DO SO

Total Questions: 35 | Time: 1 hr.

## Guidelines for the Candidate

1. You will get additional ten minutes to fill up information about yourself on the OMR Sheet, before the start of the exam.
2. Write your **Name, School Code, Class, Roll No.** and **Mobile Number** clearly on the **OMR Sheet** and do not forget to sign it. We will share your marks / result and other information related to SOF exams on your mobile number.
3. The Question Paper comprises three sections:

   **Logical Reasoning** (5 Questions), **Computers and Information Technology** (25 Questions) and **Achievers Section** (5 Questions).

   Each question in Achievers Section carries 2 marks, whereas all other questions carry one mark each.
4. All questions are compulsory. There is no negative marking. Use of calculator is not permitted.
5. There is only ONE correct answer. Choose only ONE option for an answer.
6. To mark your choice of answers by darkening the circles on the OMR Sheet, use **HB Pencil** or **Blue / Black ball point pen** only. E.g.

   **Q.16: _____ means to hold down the left mouse button while you move the mouse pointer to a new place.**

   A. Single click B. Double click C. Dragging D. Left click

   As the correct answer is option C, you must darken the circle corresponding to option C on the OMR Sheet.

   16. Ⓐ Ⓑ ● Ⓓ
7. Rough work should be done in the blank space provided in this booklet.
8. Return the OMR Sheet to the invigilator at the end of the exam.
9. Please fill in your personal details in the space provided on this page before attempting the paper.

SOF

SCIENCE OLYMPIAD FOUNDATION

Inspiring Young Minds Through Knowledge Olympiads

Name:..........................................................................................................

SOF Olympiad Roll No.:.......................................................... Contact No.:..........................................................

1. Which of the following options will complete the given pattern?

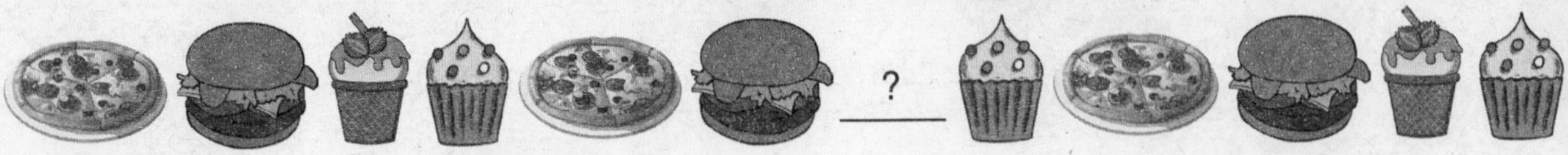


A.  B.  C.  D. 

2. Tree _______ is the tallest.

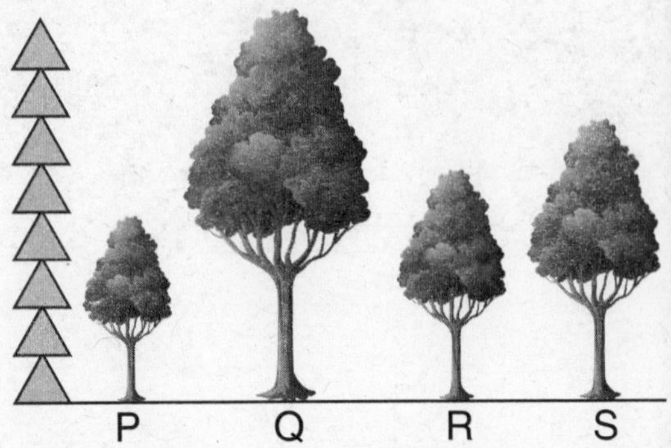


A. P

B. Q

C. R

D. S

3. Which of the following objects can be used to draw a square?

A.  B.  C.  D. 

4. Select the odd one out.

A.  B.  C.  D. 

5. There are _______ slanting lines in the given figure.

A. 8

B. 10

C. 19

D. 12

SPACE FOR ROUGH WORK

6. Identify the following.
   - It looks like a box that contains the glass surface known as screen.
   - It is used to display text and images.

   A.  B.  C.  D. 

---

7. Which of the following devices contains ON/OFF button that provides power to the computer?

   A. Keyboard B. Mouse C. CPU D. Printer

---

8. Which of the following statements is INCORRECT while working on computer?

   A. You should keep your back straight while working on a computer.
   B. You must sit too close to the computer.
   C. You should avoid eating and drinking while working on a computer.
   D. You should not touch any part of computer with wet hands.

---

9. Which of the following parts of computer is capable of moving arrow/pointer across the screen?

   A.  B.  C.  D. 

---

10. Identify the following.
    - It is a watch that you can wear on your wrist.
    - It can perform all the tasks, done by a smartphone.

    A. Smartwatch B. Intelligent-wrist
    C. Smartwrist D. Smarthand

---

11. In offices computers can be used to ________.

    A. Watch movies and listen to music B. Generate marksheets of the students
    C. Keep record of all the patients D. Maintain information of employees

---

SPACE FOR ROUGH WORK

12. Which of the following parts of a computer resembles its layout with the typewriter?

A. 

B. 

C. 

D. 

13. Which of the following keys is used to type the given sentence in upper case?

COMPUTER IS AN ELECTRONIC MACHINE

A. 

B. 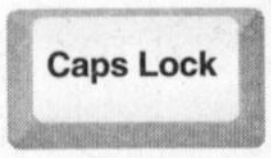


C. 

D. 

14. Which of the following is NOT an alphabet key?

A. 

B. 

C. 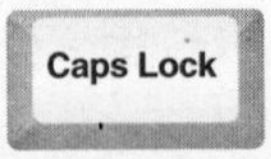


D. 

15. With the help of which part of computer, the Shut down option is selected in Start menu?

A. 

B. 

C. 

D. 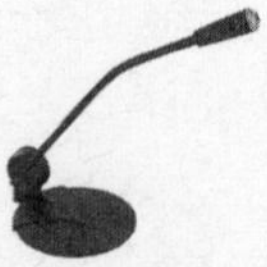

16. Which of the following computers is bigger in size and difficult to move from one place to another?

A. 

B. 

C. 

D. 

17. Computer helps you to draw pictures. Which of the following options shows this?

A. 

B. 

C. 

D. 

SPACE FOR ROUGH WORK

18. The action of ending all activities and closing the computer is called ______ process.

A. Shut down B. Start up C. Switching D. Resting

---

19. Which of the following shapes is NOT used to draw the given picture in MS-Paint?

A.  B.  C.  D. 

---

20. Which of the following devices allows you to chat with your friend by means of video calls?

A.  B.  C.  D. 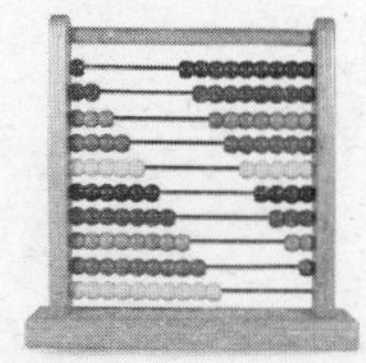

---

21. Which of the following parts of computer is NOT necessarily required while playing a video game on it?

A. Monitor B. CPU C. Printer D. Mouse

---

22. Which of the following is a man-made machine and does not work on fuel?

A.  B.  C.  D. 

---

23. Which of the following devices can be used to withdraw money from a person's bank account?

A.  B.  C. 

D. 

SPACE FOR ROUGH WORK

24. In which of the following places computers are used to play games?

A. 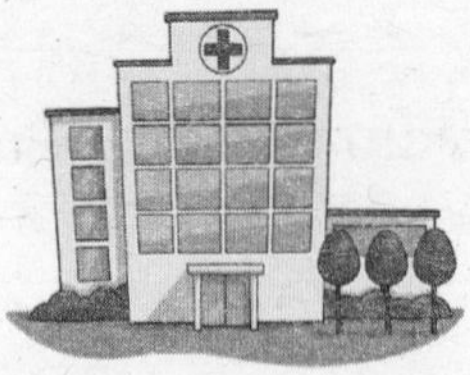

B. 

C. 

D. 

25. Riya is using a device that is allowing her to use her fingers to move pictures from one place to another. Which of the following options makes this task possible?

A. Touch screen B. Fine screen C. Picture screen D. Flat screen

26. Which of the following CANNOT be considered as the part of a computer mouse?

A. Left button B. Right button C. Display screen D. Scroll wheel

27. Which of the following shapes CANNOT be drawn using oval tool of MS-Paint?

A.  B.  C.  D. 

28. Which of the following is NOT available as a ready-made shape in MS-Paint?

A.  B. 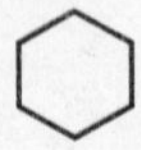 C. 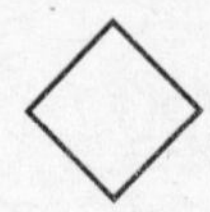 D. 

29. Which of the following keys when pressed, will allow you to display the '^' sign on monitor screen?

A. 

B. 

C. 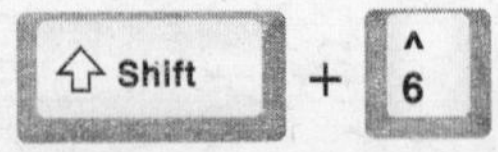


D. 

30. Which of the following does NOT require electricity to work with?

A. 

B. 

C. 

D. 

SPACE FOR ROUGH WORK

31. To start a computer, you should first switch on the main power supply. Which of the following options represents the CORRECT next required step to follow?
   A. Switch on the power button located on CPU.
   B. Switch on the power button located on monitor.
   C. Switch on the power button located on keyboard.
   D. Switch on the power button located on mouse.

32. Which of the following options will convert the Picture-1 into Picture-2 as shown in the given image of MS-Paint?

Picture-1 Picture-2

A.  B.  C.  D. 

33. Which of the following parts of a computer mouse marked as P, Q, R and S can be used to move the document or picture up or down on the computer screen?
   A. P
   B. Q
   C. R
   D. S

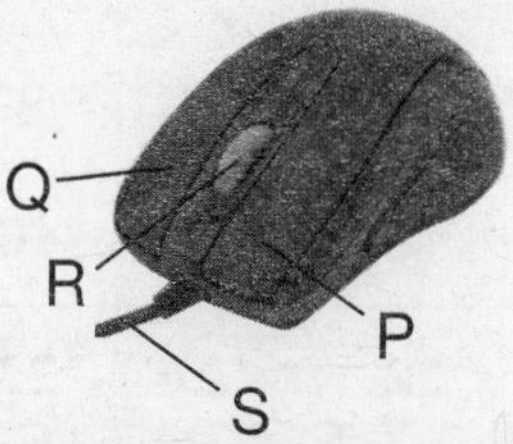


34. Palak has performed following sequence of tasks using keyboard:
   1. Pressed [* 8]
   2. Pressed [Caps Lock]
   3. Pressed [I]
   4. Pressed [Caps Lock]
   5. Pressed [N] [D] [I] [A]

   What would be the result of these actions? (Assume that caps lock key was off initially.)
   A. 8India B. *india C. 8indiA D. 8INDIA

SPACE FOR ROUGH WORK

35. Select the CORRECT statement about laptop computer.

A. It is small in size, so you can easily keep it in your pocket.

B. It is required to be placed on a desk to work with and can't move easily.

C. It can be used during travelling.

D. It does not work on battery.

SPACE FOR ROUGH WORK

## ANSWER KEYS

| | | | | | | | | | | | | | |
|---|---|---|---|---|---|---|---|---|---|---|---|---|---|
| 1. | (C) | 2. | (B) | 3. | (D) | 4. | (A) | 5. | (B) | 6. | (A) | 7. | (C) |
| 8. | (B) | 9. | (B) | 10. | (A) | 11. | (D) | 12. | (B) | 13. | (B) | 14. | (C) |
| 15. | (A) | 16. | (B) | 17. | (A) | 18. | (A) | 19. | (D) | 20. | (A) | 21. | (C) |
| 22. | (A) | 23. | (C) | 24. | (C) | 25. | (A) | 26. | (C) | 27. | (D) | 28. | (D) |
| 29. | (C) | 30. | (D) | 31. | (A) | 32. | (A) | 33. | (C) | 34. | (A) | 35. | (C) |




SOF SCIENCE OLYMPIAD FOUNDATION

**National Office:** Plot 99, First Floor, Sector 44 Institutional area, Gurugram -122 003 (HR) India

Email: info@sofworld.org | Website: www.sofworld.org

Regd. Office: 406, Taj Apt., Ring Road, New Delhi-110 029

*Note: Please address all communication to the National Office only.*